THE VIOLENT WEST

THE VIOLENT WEST

poems by

ZULFIKAR GHOSE

MACMILLAN

SBN boards: 333 13241 6
SBN paper: 333 13613 6

First published 1972 by
MACMILLAN AND CO LTD
London and Basingstoke
Associated companies in New York Toronto
Dublin Melbourne Johannesburg & Madras

Printed in Great Britain by
LOWE AND BRYDONE (PRINTERS) LTD
LONDON

CONTENTS

I Westward Flight

II A Private Lot

III Tyrannies

Acknowledgements
Some of these poems were broadcast by the B.B.C. Third Pro-
gramme. Others were first published in *Encounter, Hudson
Review, New Statesman, New York Times, New York Times
Book of Verse, Outposts, Pakistan Quarterly, Poetry* and
Transatlantic Review.

'View from the Observatory' first appeared in *Poetry*,
© Modern Poetry Association 1971.

I

WESTWARD FLIGHT

THE POET AT LAKE TRAVIS

The old harmonies meet
like migrating fowl descending to drink
at this lake's edge and become transient
       settlers. I'm foolish to think
              such argument
will hold water; but the music whose beat

       this stillness adumbrates,
the music which swells like northward-bound sails
and shouts with the short jabs of finches' flights,
       oh, it's false; worse, it fails
              to make days nights
which go on and on as in a long-haul jet's

       westward flight. Only choose
to think so, I who begin in falsehood,
fouled-up vision. For this landscape
       of wooded slopes that should
              distort lines, shape
a subtler aesthetic of greens and blues,

       be what the slick mind makes
of it, insists on the harsh independence
of its constituents. I see fragments, bits:
       gone that vivid violence,
              and gone, gone its
terrors. And so this music at the lake's

3

edge persists like a pimp —
solicitation's sneer and mockery! Wrong,
everything wrong. I suffer reversals,
rejecting what has long
held conviction. A false
start, a baby-cry, come, old cheater, dump

it all into the lake's
garbage-can mouth, for look the butterflies
scan the prosody of flowers, and you! *You?*
Ask Mr Berryman why his
bones ache, why few
faltering rise, why only a Maker makes.

THE PURSUIT OF FROST

Wandering again, come
to this shore, observing the severe
disenchantment of water which remains
anonymous and clear:
cleanse what stains
here and trumpet which purity a welcome

through arches of the mind?
All this and crushed like aluminium cans,
like burnt-out fires a black patch left, smokers'
lungs on the shore. All runs
to neglect, to wreckers'
yards goes all where metal-chewing machines grind

up a culture. Carbon waste,
that's all of the air expelled. A seismograph
needle, that's all, as if gaudy Broadway were granite
that heaved. But enough, enough.
Wandering, can it
be as with bird-migrations − to taste

the warm waters and to move
on always ahead of the cold-front, flying
from the pursuit of frost? What assaults
landscapes then, conferring
on evergreens a false
permanence? The eye remembers, does not reprove

the mind but only feasts
on new possibilities. Here, and here, establish
settlement or dynasty or whatever satisfies
vanity. Have your wish,
wanderer, for butterflies
will soon go south and the fabulous beasts

will return to their god-
forsaken mythologies, reviving terror.
Broken glass and fragmented pottery, underground
cables and what error not on error
compounded: a lost-and-found
civilization (a home, wanderer!), an ancient fraud.

IT'S YOUR LAND, BOSS

On a hillside in Texas,
digging the brown earth to deliver like calves
the limestone rocks with which it bulged, I thought:
    The stubborn earth survives
      more than the periodic drought
and the seasonal rainstorm; but how affects us

the word, O Earth, we call,
stooping, when like pilgrims we come to a land,
packaged across the turbulent air in the paths of jets!
    A T.V. feature, canned
      for syndication, that's
the prophet's dramatic way: to come home and fall

on his knees with an at last
finality, seeing salvation in a handful of earth.
I think of Israel and of the Jews who kill
    and die for it, the land worth
      the idea they fulfil
with their dying, an absolute belief and trust

that the earth has a mother's
claim to patriotic rites and sacrificial feasts.
The coarse, porous earth, toothy with flints,
    casting out mythological beasts,
      cynically hints
that it might actually be soulless. Let others

7

define whose perceptions
don't pickaxe the soil. I have more on my mind.
There's the grave mystique, too, compelling the youth
 of America to find
  primitive versions of truth,
to lose itself in flowery misconceptions,

  wearing homespun cloth and beads;
or to stand before microphones on a college campus
and declare its own peculiar allegiance
 to the earth. And thus,
  whether it makes sense
or not, a revolutionary rhetoric breeds

  a counter-rhetoric's pretentious
slogans: *America — Love It or Leave It,* and so on.
Earth-kissing Zionists aside (and each country
 is an Israel for someone),
  people don't really
care nowadays for sentimental gestures,

  for sacredness is suspect,
the earth more a problem for conservation than
a banner across a jingoist breast, and the land
 merely a real estate speculation.
  Countries, countries! Brand-
names, faded and disfigured, on the wrecked

  product that builds up rust
among the weeds and wild flowers growing high behind
the idle farms. Worms and beetle-like insects
 and the burrowing animals find
  a home in the wreck's
corrugations. Old mother earth's a heap of dust.

My temporary peasant fervour
plays out its fantasy on the Texas hillside.
I'm not sure what this earth means to me.
I don't take the peasant's pride
in the quality
of the soil. I don't need to. But feel poorer

because of this loss,
this irrelevance. I rake aside the stones, push
at a rock that's too heavy to move. I throw
away tufts of grass. From this lush
land, too, I must go
towards horizons which the jet-liners cross.

THE VIOLENT WEST

I drive in south Texas where
the land is as flat as the Punjab and grows
cotton and citrus fruits. I could not be closer
to whatever my instinct knows
to be home. The mimosa,
the bougainvillea, palms, sugarcane, all share

this soil with India.
When tropical storms hit the Gulf coast
the rain in Austin could come from an eastern sky.
It would seem that here's the best
compromise, a land of my
childhood which speaks the language of my mind: here,

so close to home, still I think
of London: to walk on Barnes Common or Putney Heath
in May when chestnut trees make England dear;
to stand by the Thames at Hammersmith
beside the borough's dahlia
and rose bushes, how can such gestures horizons shrink,

how can sentiments a people change?
To observe a commitment to the plants is insufficient,
for there's the subtler falsehood (ah, what resolves
paradox and contradiction!)
that wraps the mind with a shawl's
warmth and makes the skin itch. Ha! Exchange

charity with silence, like Lear,
as if the mind were the chamber of a pistol
and the skin grew protective thorns. Explosions,
  as if nuclear devices still
   tested those portions
of the mind which had not yet become a Nevada,

  only that, only that.
In summer the sky over Texas goes wild at sunset,
the billowing earth blows its hot breath at the west
  making the iron-grey clouds melt
   into the fiercest
red, the chicken-hawk turns into a still silhouette

  against the day's last blue
before swooping towards the violent west from where
the little birds, cardinals and finches, fly to
  their chosen darkness. On summer
   nights the possum and the armadillo
come down from the wooded hills, skunks slip into

  shadows, but each is drawn
to the fatal highway where westward travellers drive
towards dreams. The Spaniard came to Texas once
  in search òf gold, alive
   with hopes for the brilliance
of Peru, of Mexico. Not even water in the brown

  dust of the western desert
he found. The land is greener now, civilized,
settled by immigrants who fled from war
  and persecution, glorified Christ
   in a thousand timber
churches and sent the native to his death:

11

in my mind the wearisome
repetitions transmit the videotape of sequences
well rehearsed and truthfully acted of the first
displacement, the lost sense
of belonging: and with a burst
as in Nevada's sky, back the confusions come.

AN IMPERIAL EDUCATION

The P. & O. liner docked in Tilbury
and I who'd been looking for Wordsworth's landscapes
(since the old Empire still educated the new India)
        saw instead the blurred shapes
            of a wet April day: a drear
England appeared of cranes, warehouses and silvery

        railway tracks. At London
    Bridge, I leaned over the murky, embittered
Thames, taking an old-fashioned Eng. Lit. view,
        not seeing the littered
            river but some dew-
drenched willow branches hanging over a sylvan

        stream a Blackie textbook
    had made me long for in a Bombay classroom.
I walked the streets of London with a pensive
        face, a posture assumed
            from some page in *Palgrave*
or a Millais reproduction, calculated to look

        similar to the shepherds
    returning from the meadows of their offices
to their bedsitting cottages in South Ken.
        All my suits were three-piece
            pinstripe with a red carnation
in the buttonhole. Swallows were all the birds

13

I saw, daffodils all
the flowers. I wouldn't drink beer because I'd
been told that young men only drank sherry.
A Byron from Bombay, I sighed,
looked sad and world-weary.
Peter Sellers' Indian was less comical

than my rendering
of English customs. The naïve, confused
and clueless East died slowly. Imitative
and sycophantic, used
to a century of submissive
bowing, the Indian, always when *'God Save the King'*

was played, stood more erect
than the Englishman. That and Macaulay
were my education. Now I wonder what immigrants
arriving in Southall say
about their long acquaintance
with the English way of life which they must suspect

of a subtle corruption,
being run by Fagins and Artful Dodgers. Well,
dear English reader, know that whether it's Delhi's
sudden dismissal
of the B.B.C., or Shelley's
words in my mouth, it's all due to Imperial Education.

THE BUTTERFLY

Beside Lake Travis when
autumn in the north sent butterflies to the pines
and live-oaks of Texas, their rayon wings printed
with *art nouveau* designs
transparent against the splintered
light (the sun a million fire-flies), there, then,

beside the lake, during
that moment of seeing the yellow wings held
up like colour-slides, hundreds of them among
yellow flowers, and compelled
then to watch a power-boat which flung
its sporting girl to my sight, bikini-bosom luring

the eye as its cleavage
cleaved through the water, I noticed,
turning back to the flowers, the butterflies gone
high into the air, and so missed
the chance to catch one;
but observed, just then, obscure in the cage

of flowers and leaves,
a perfect specimen: black-winged and swallow-tailed,
with russet spots, it was lovelier and rarer
(holding colloquy with the blue-petalled
flower) than common lepidoptera:
I could have caught it with the greatest of ease

15

      and its perfection
praised and preserved with love − instead I watched
it face the flower like a woman a mirror, hated
     my lust and walked away: wretched
        as at a loss, and elated
as if the girl in the speedboat were my companion.

ALL YOU NEED

Love's become frivolous,
flaunted as a formula for universal peace,
a message from pop enterprises; it can't,
surely, be any of these,
nor can it grant
general panaceas. Love's not a generous

millionaire with an eye
on tax deductions. Off-season roses wrapped
in cellophane won't make the enemy cede
an inch; nor will the slapped
face calmly proceed
to preach love. No one, apparently, will buy

love as a settlement
for wrong or loss or hurt or grievance.
And the desire — as you pursue some clichéd
version of romance —
to lie under the shade
of an elm in summer beside an elegant

river which breeds
no mosquitoes but supposedly flows
like Chopin and to have in your arms the glossy young
beauty from *Vogue* whose
willingness among
the butterflies and the dots of sunlight exceeds

        your immediate purpose,
ah, lover, what cinematic ecstasy might not
be yours! Or take the other, the one who thrives
        on excluding all thought
           of promiscuity and lives
on devotion and would rather his bones decomposed

        before be changed his mind:
such faith, lover, comes cheap from the Woolworth
paperbacks. But these private anxieties aside,
        what's left of love? Birth,
           copulation and death ride
still their strict tyranny over mankind

        while on and on we rant
about *Love, love, love.* The popular song
at the top of the disc-jockey's sacred charts
        compels the eager young
           to lose their silly hearts
and their money, but merely fills their minds with cant.

COME, SAILOR

Not by journeying,
Odysseus (since to you the Mediterranean's
currents are erratic, violent mysteries),
        not fresh explorations
            now amidst the swollen seas,
Odysseus, will bring back the heart-soothing

        vision, nor will the hills
again be purple near the town that was once
home; and sooner will the extinct birds rise
        in imagined migrations
            before your startled eyes
than your searching discover the particles

        of dust become again
compacted into masonry, the walls and domes
of fallen cities. Open gutters and sewers
        ran out of those kingdoms
            whose golden towers
only are remembered, and the fields of yellow corn

        were sometimes black
with locusts. The hills of Rome, the isles
of Greece, even there, Odysseus. And still,
        when you stand beside the sails
            and look down at the tall
waves shouldering your ship, there, Odysseus, like

a drowned sailor
a body floats, its face yours and mine. Compulsive,
this voyaging — as if the next calm will settle
the sea-spray and drive
away the clouds until
the horizon offers the choice of a natural harbour

where intermingled come
scents of thyme and rosemary, or a clearer
perspective of the ocean's routes, each one
an illusion that nearer
is that vision
which makes sons slam doors on their parents' home.

Chill breezes catalogue
again autumn's severities; the sky hurries eastward
and the gulls ride a swifter wind. The seas
twitch, and again the voice you heard
in ancient mythologies
calls: Come, sailor, journey towards the cold fog.

COWBOYS IN BERKSHIRE

And nor will the saints stare
with that look of accusation and profound wisdom,
standing under the shade of cypress trees on a hill
where peasants and fishermen come,
open-mouthed and gullible,
nor will they lift all-embracing arms, nor their

solemn voices raise in
benediction or censure. Art columnists prophesy
that icons from St Petersburg are good investment,
and already prices are high.
Candles at the elegant
dinner, the lights switched off, there's reason

in deliberate retreat
apparently. Or the intellectual's late conversion,
a dialogue on one's knees, alone in the pew's
hard oak, with one's own
mind. What substitutes
for crossword puzzles and Latin epigrams, the neat

filling out of empty
spaces? Executives at weekends wear western
costumes and play cowboys in Berkshire, riding hard
and shooting with a certain
aim. A cynical regard
for Time, that's all, which must be given a lofty,

       idealised fulfilment.
A saint's invective sends a cypress tree
shuddering, the words would draw dark clouds down
      from a sky which supposedly
        is prepared to wear God's frown
and to mimic God's tongue, and with what astonishment

      a populace kneels!
Down in the valley, in the flour-mill by the river,
clocked-in workers keep oiled the expensive plant.
      The sermons the saints deliver
        on the hill aren't
going to change the modern dogma, for miracles

      are irrelevant when jets
land cargoes of fruit at Heathrow in the worst
winter. We work like saints and serve the state,
      convinced that civilization's cursed
        or that we can still cultivate
it like a prize rose: we've become our own prophets.

VIEW FROM THE OBSERVATORY

Through dark space, measurable
only in light-years, as if penetrating the surface
of an ocean one saw little silver fish glow in a dance
   and turn the liquid space
      into twinkling fluorescence,
suddenly appeared the distant stars: the visible

   thus transcends belief,
and the years are reduced to the bleep-bleep
of radio signals. Vega quivered at the centre,
   turning green and then deep
      blue, not a bright star
at all, but a mass of self-contradiction, a thief

   of its own identity.
How the years go! Dispersed in space like smoke,
reaching farther than a telescope can retrieve.
   The distant stars provoke
      a theology: we should believe
more than we see. And yet the recalcitrant naked eye

   wearily contracts its pupil
from such grey-haired wisdom, seeking only the delight
of surprise. Pocked with craters, the moon appeared,
   full of October, I thought, bright
      as over the Pacific, smeared
and streaked with sweat. But no, a simple,

            unpoetical moon, closer
to its own truth, masked with a topography
that veined and hollowed its bloated opulence.
            But there's no truth in it if I
                close my eyes, no sense
beyond the starry explosions in the inner

            darkness, none at all,
the sputterings of colour, the delicate flames
which burn the inside of eyelids, the flares
            at their blinding games
                in the charred sockets. There's
wisdom in sudden illuminations! Sparks fall

            from fireworks as easily
as stars from a heaven the astronomer builds
like a pointillist adding more and more dots
            until the stretched space fills
                up and a new perspective creates
a new illusion for which the telescope is busily

            aimed to the precise minute.
We may agree on a world with open eyes but
the rebel years will tear up any treaty between
            states of mind and shut
                to the eye any vision
that does not excitedly see the infinite.

WHERE THE WATERS DARKEN

If we finally
like cancer patients seek out those remedies
which, like radioactive bombardment of the collar
        bone that attempts to freeze
            the cellular
multiplication while at the same time possibly

        destroys the tissues
and corrodes the bone to allow the heart a brief
continuation — O such extremities, such desperate
        delayings of grief
            we simply have to mate
with, the thighs violent and the nails jealous

        of flesh that cushions
the backbone and the mouth more willing to devour
the breast's fullness than air, the sharp air
        of mountains, or
            the sea's terror
in the flecks of sea-spray, the cold relations

        of ancient animosities,
the sea and the mountain, the desert and the forest,
if finally it must come to negations, and heads
        that shake are the greyest
            on their acknowledged death-beds,
what use then the brutish freedom and tyranny's

                    indulgent withdrawal
of the whip? Brochures of tourist-land, white
crescents of beaches and blue Kodakchrome
                    skies offer a packaged flight
                        to elsewhere from home:
we're nations on calendars, we're the pictorial

                    ads of the air lines,
pursuing conservation programmes, restoring
the weathered and war-damaged masonry
                    of cathedrals and pouring
                        an exaggerated energy
into traditional pageants as if illusions

                    are a sufficient
defence. Hold the tanned waist between
the bikini-bosom and the briefs at the hips,
                    lover on the beach where the green
                        sea with its iron-grey ships
is darkening its waters, gently now when

                    light diminishes
at midday. Walk softly, lovers, among the shells
which pebble the sand, linger beside the waves
                    where swooping seagulls
                        peck at the day's
broken-glass reflections. Distorted dimensions

                    of space, and soot like cells
in corrupted tissues while the jets rev
towards the economy resorts. As if the final
                    attempt to survive
                        this terminal
disease is pitiably to cry: What else, what else!

THE OTHER WORLD

The long road I took
south along the coast, the ocean springing
up with its surprising sunsets, this
and that other evening,
and then lost in a mist,
its greying blue gashed with the last vermilion streak

that evening and this,
the ocean submerged beyond the humpbacked hills
each with its solitary cactus; all reduced
now to bare symbols
in a confused
cinematic projection of which the mind must witness

successive screenings.
The Pacific or the Atlantic, who knows now
the ocean's name? Pines or palms, what trees,
desert sand or northern snow,
journeys, journeys,
and bright-feathered birds with clipped wings,

here and not here,
as if I looked again at the same photograph,
a repetitious returning to an obsessive scrutiny,
dream or the narrow shaft
of consciousness where tiny
dots of light expand and contract as from a projector

                    until they focus
into worn masonry. Past the cathedrals rising
out of the fog, past the whitewashed churches in
                    the sun where the peasants bring
                              fruit. Over the wooden
bridge and the concrete viaduct. Through the dust

                    at the bullocks' heels
and past the temples giddily standing in their heavy
incensed air, travelling south along the coast,
                    never far from the very
                              edge of the world: cursed
to this motion, driven more than driving: the wheels

                    silent on the tarmac.
And stopping each night at the same motel where
the thin-lipped porter serves next morning's breakfast
                    and, pocketing his tip, wishes me fare-
                              well when I haste
away, making an early start. The ocean, pock-marked

                    with light, keeps its
distance, but already evening falls and there are miles
to go yet and the night-frost begins to fasten
                    itself to the earth and the hills
                              are loud with crickets and I hasten
towards the retreating point where the beam hits

                    some furry fugitive.
The severe abstraction of darkness, the massed
solidity of water, air which exhausts the lungs.
                    Where the cockatoo is crazed,
                              the snake hisses. Where among
silent colonies of ants the burdened beasts live.

II

A PRIVATE LOT

COMING HERE

Flat land, empty even of cactus
and high flying birds; not desert sand

nor the dry, cracked earth, but the floor
of a furnace in which the sun is forged;

not yellow nor brown under the relentless
risings; quiet as still ponds in dark

weather, the lilies limp under the threat
of thunder in high humidity;

or as on a flight to another continent,
the tedious speed of the long hours

slow as a paralytic taking a step;
dull grey of old cannons this land,

haze its only connection with the sky.
Did you come here, my friends,

leaving the flower-strewn graves
or the petal-lipped urns? Ah,

my desperate visitors! Where
there's not shade enough at noon

for a snake; where night falls
without the flying birds carrying

31

on the tips of their wings the fiery sun;
where no D.D.T. was necessary

to destroy the mosquito;
where vultures are extinct.

IN THE DESERT

When grandma took me to Quetta
the train cut through sugarcane
and maize fields across the Punjab
and entered the Thar desert.

I stood at the window for hours
and watched the sand of the desert
meet the sandy beach of the sky
where the heat-haze broke in waves.

It was the first time that I'd seen
a world in which there seemed
nothing to live for and nothing
with which to keep one alive.

I had a fantasy as children do
of being alone in the desert
and lasting there for no longer
than a drop of water.

I stood at the window for hours
and wanted to know for how long
the world as far as I could see
would continue completely empty.

Now thirty years later when I look back
on that journey through the desert
I feel I am still at the window
searching the horizon for plants.

ISLANDERS

Like water-buffalo worrying the mud-bank
of a river where the tongue can't reach
deep enough into the veins of the cracked

earth for water; or in the monsoon
months when the land sinks —
such alternatives! As with those other

islanders, cultivating the slopes
of volcanic hills, on the lip of fire,
the murderous vicinity of violence:

so on the edge of this ocean whose seas
whip our chained islands: we live
where we're most vulnerable to death.

THE BREAK-DOWN

To break down — as once on the borders
of Mato Grosso — and to discover
that even the rivers are hostile.

After the rains, the road heaped
with its own rubble, a world war
avenue in Coventry or Dresden.

The twilight swarmed down the sky
with the descent of insects,
the fur of black velvet, thick

as moss on the river-bank.
And irritations that reach the bone.
On the far side of ranches

each larger than Yorkshire beside
the jungle that rehearses
Amazonia. With night the fire-flies

plucked at the throat of the little
air that humidity had not choked.
To break down there as if arriving

at a determined terminal
and, looking at the jungle the next
morning, to expect no rescue.

4 A.M. TRAFFIC

I hear lorries speeding on
the Great West Road, bound
I suppose for Smithfield or
Covent Garden. To hell

with this insomnia!
I gaze at books on a shelf,
the works of poets who've gone
far towards achievement.

I hear a plane take-off
from Heathrow, a Boeing
which need not descend
before Los Angeles.

Such stamina for distance!
I sit drinking wine, smoking;
I sit imagining other
people's destinations;

and their ability to arrive.

ARRIVING LATE

My correspondents wrote confirming
what I read also in the travel books
that it was a green land whose southern
provinces were famous for their vineyards;

in the north the apples were crisper
and sweeter than candied peanuts,
and one harvest of corn in the central
region was worth more than the Incas' gold.

I arrived during an exceptional winter
when frost destroyed the citrus orchards
in the south where the valleys had
previously trapped a sub-tropical sun.

A hasty harvest has sent the corn prices up;
the north suffers power-cuts and unemployment.
I'm told that if I'd come a season earlier
I would have seen how rich the land was:

AT SOME EXTREMITY

On the farthest point of
a promontory, the land so low that
it must at high tide be submerged.

In the pine-forest, too, when snow
which covers the wolf's footsteps
confounds all evidence with a white alibi.

Or in an anonymous apartment
on the twentieth floor where the
doorstep has accumulated a month's mail.

And one hears of a shotgun
accidentally going off
in a wood, in some lonely cottage.

Where else shall I look for you,
my friend? Once I leaned over
a bank where willows arched

across the river and in the still,
green water I thought that
the face I clearly saw was yours.

A FLIGHT

In the end, then, is that all?
After the meticulous preparation
of itineraries for the successive
journeys, the advance bookings.

A room with a bed and a side table.
The squalor of air terminals
where the dishevelled transit
passengers wait for connections.

A room with a bed, the sheets
freshly laundered, and a side table.
The flights across continents
over a Sahara or an Atlantic

and fuel stops in the early hours
somewhere on the edge of Africa —
Dakar or Monrovia — where no one
leaves or joins the flight.

A room with a bed and a side table.
To walk on beaches, to visit
the hedonistic centres of the new
metropolis, to tour the interior

and to find the jungle which
had been cut back encroach again
upon the vacant spaces, renewing
a claustrophobic darkness. And then?

A room with a bed, the sheets
creased and disturbed, the body's
raging finally quietened, even
the sweat dried up, the brow cold,

and on the side table an empty
glass beside the little labelled
bottle which, too, is empty, the air
gone stale with cigarette smoke.

AT A DIFFICULT TIME

When the Olympic athlete whose body
we'd applauded comes down with cancer;

when the ski run
is overwhelmed by an avalanche;

when —
oh, what the hell . . . .

Banal antitheses,
what else? Such breathlessness, ha!

The gaudy antibiotics like beads
to give the savages of the interior.

What else?
Marathon runners in the floodlit stadium.

A race is coming to an end.
Fuck it.

41

OLD RAGGED CLAWS

What land is this from where two poets exiled
themselves? Barbarism knocks its bull's head
and sends the continents drifting, and not here
only is the beast burdensome. What land is this?

Once I used to travel with no expectation
than surprise, wanting only rivers to be wide
and plains to spread their vineyards and corn
with a deep green and for the sky to be

on its best blue behaviour. Now I read cautionary
guides and consult a travel agency about
the quality of the bathrooms before going.
Age makes cowards of us as youth makes fools.

I should have sat behind a yoke binding the bullocks
to the earth and let the sun bully my head
into submission: scratching the hard, neutral soil,
bound by horizons which the tropical haze held

in its sweaty palm. I feel still my arm-pits weep,
and dust afflict my larynx like a drought.
My voice still creaks like a bullock-cart
pursuing its wobbly ruts, and my eyes are shot

with the blood of sunsets that brought no rest.
Gone that land, slipped away with the earth's kicking
its heels, its trees uprooted for the desert's
pleasure, for the desert's thirst its rivers emptied.

Under this wintry sun trapped among wanton clouds,
at this junction of migratory routes where I
watch birds fill up a tree for an hour and then leave
it empty as a football stadium, what land is this

where fields are banked with rusting refrigerators
and beautification programmes, bringing cosmetics
to geography, fill up the earth's wrinkles with lakes?
I have come so far West, the East is near.

A PRIVATE LOT

The old wagon-train trail is still
marked in the valley, a stony,
axle-creaking track in the pine
forest, so lumped with limestone that
one imagines the wheels wobble;

the trail ends against massed boulders
while a mile away is the clear
alternative of a river
and a plain with a horizon
not bounded by a horseshoe hill

steeply banked with stunted pines.
To come here is to reach nowhere;
yet the track suggests the trail
was well used, not mistakenly
followed once by people who lost

their way. The realtor narrates
this bit of Texan lore and starts
to persuade me that I should build
in the privacy of these pines
a home I would not want to leave.

III

TYRANNIES

PROFESSORS MAY EXPECT TYRANNY

The girl students on the campus
have decided that they are
the most liberated generation
and have said goodbye to the bra

except for those whose favourite book
is the one with Daddy's cheques,
these adopt the latest fashions
with which to display their sex.

Pity the middle-aged professor
who's trying hard to keep alert,
for the girl rapidly taking notes
is wobbling behind her shirt

while Daddy's Girl in the front row
as if at a party surrounded by guests
gives him her undivided attention
and a view of her divided breasts.

DON'T FORGET THE PILL, DEAR

Blessed are the savage lands of this world,
the hot centres, the direct links with
the sun, or the steely icicled North,
its bared wolves' teeth at one's heart;

for observe in temperate climates, in Kew,
say, the museum-clutter of trees and the ducks
splashing in the decorative lakes: ah,
the turnstile's threepenny bit of nature!

So, we assume love's strained capacities,
maintaining the gutter's respect for the street.
The sand, the snow — such extremities of
abstract assertion while here we're surrounded

by polystyrene insulated walls and the *objets
d'art* picked up in a foreign market or on some beach;
we make spring-mattressed love with its
Kleenex anti-climax, hearing the planes descend.

Sometimes I say: *To hell with it!* For
what better declaration than to applaud
when you dance like a blizzard or become
the essence of humidity in a rain-forest?

A falsification, a trick of the cultivated mind!
A *nouvelle vague* posturing or a drugstore paperback
romance I at other times think is all
that's left. The city soot which dissipates

48

the sun, and the fumes from the gas boiler
commit us to degeneration. Gentle cowards,
our emotions muddied with restraint, we submit
to history's fashionable misconceptions.

A WOMAN'S ILLNESS

Now in mid-June she can lie
beside the apple-tree believing that
the sun restores what the antibiotics,
exploding in her blood all winter, took
from her flesh, pounds of it,
her body a hostage to recovery.

Once in November she cried
the pain out, holding my hand. I was straw
to her near-drowning. I was an oxygen mask
she needed at the peak of pain. Her breath
broke down, her face crumpled
like metal on collision.

This was the winter of
miraculous surgery. She heard about it,
a cripple reading about the Olympic Games.
Of course in her own heart she knew what
she needed most: a more demonstratively
loving son than I had been.

DISFIGURATION

The waters of your body are murky.
You bite at the air as if it hung there
like fruit. I look at the chart, the jerky
op-art line of fluctuating temperature.

You say: water hurts your teeth when you drink.
A bite of food blows you up like a balloon.
You're draining away on the bed's white enamel sink.
I give you sips of water with a spoon.

I look round the ward with half-shut eyes. Beds
seem to be hanging from the walls, coloured
by abstract faces: pale pinks, violent reds.
And when I look at you, it is as I feared:

you are a collage of what you were, torn
with pain. You are a doodle, a pretty
picture disfigured. True likeness has gone
from the canvas of your identity.

THE GERANIUM MAN

Observe, from his trunk upwards,
his shirt blossom out wild as spring;
hear the insensible words,
the nasal voice with which he sings:
the world's lover, see him bow
to strangers (God, anything
and nothing are significant!),
this admirable innocent,
holy as a Hindu cow.

The budgerigar bells, the long
hair, this geranium man in his pot,
what he sings is not a song
and what he thinks is not a thought.
Blown-up poster gestures for speech
(O but his metaphysics cannot
bear words), he applauds purities
whose own ecstasy lies
in the real being out of reach.

THE LEPIDOPTERIST

Out in the state of Rio in summer
after the rains he went among sunlit
steaming hills, for it was the season
for butterflies. Cattle grazed on

the slopes, bird-cries echoed in
the valleys and even the quiet
humming-bird was absorbed in some
vibrating urgency. The mango and

the cashew trees had shed their riper
fruit. The bamboo trees bowed. The sun
like a restored monarch threw newly
minted coins with his own image

at the earth which shone from a million
places. The sky-high hawks swooped
and soared again; the emergent ants
assembled for their lethal parades.

Butterflies hovered entranced
above fragrant bushes, peacock
blue or orange with black circular
markings. He caught them, killed them

and later framed each in a glass case:
wings stretched, body pinned, the type
labelled. The rains would return and
extinction, too, was a possibility.

THE ANT AND THE MOSQUITO

Followers of strict codes, policed
into one-way systems, the ants
carry on their business with the least
fuss: killers, devourers of plants,
but efficient, quiet.

Urbane, civil, never a beast,
now one may stray into a bowl
of sugar, now another feast
upon a fallen fig: but ants all
are virtuously silent.

Not the mosquito, that unique
pest: kill one between clapping hands,
another comes: physically weak,
of little substance, it demands
attention, response.

It will enter the ear to speak
what one has heard it say before:
not straightforward, plain, but oblique,
devious its menace: an utter bore,
its product a disease.

THE WEST'S EMPTINESS

There's a greyness there, as if the horizon
towards which your receding body went
were the west in winter from where the storms
come. There's an emptiness there too, as if
the earth had again become flat and ended
where you left it, where any traveller must fall.

I've followed you west, gone as far as your native
Arizona. All I saw was a desert which seemed
flatter than the earth before Copernicus
and a sky gaudier than the war-paint of Indian
chiefs and the red ball of a setting sun caught
in the raised arms of a cactus; not you, not you.

THE REMOVE

The Sikh from Ambala in East Punjab,
India, formerly in the British Empire,
the Muslim from Sialkot in West Punjab,
Pakistan, formerly British India,
the Sikh boy and the Muslim boy are two
of twenty such Sikhs and Muslims
from East Punjab and West Punjab, which
formerly were the Punjab,
standing together in assembly, fearfully
miming the words of a Christian hymn.

Later, their firework voices explode
in Punjabi until Mr Iqbal —
which can be a Sikh name or a Muslim name,
Mohammed Iqbal or Iqbal *Singh* —
who comes from Jullundur in East Punjab
but near enough to the border to be almost
West Punjab, who is a specialist in
the archaic intonations of the *Raj,*
until the three-piece-suited Mr Iqbal
gives a stiff-collared voice to his
Punjabi command to shut their thick wet
lips on the scattering sparks of their
white Secondary Modern teeth.

Mr Iqbal has come to London to teach
English to Punjabi Sikhs and Muslims
and has pinned up in his class pictures
of Gandhi and Jinnah, Nehru and Ayub
in case the parents come to ask in Punjabi
how the kids are doing in English.

And so: twenty years after
the Union Jack came down on Delhi
and the Punjab became East Punjab and
West Punjab and the Sikhs did not like it
and the Muslims did not like the Sikhs
not liking it and they killed each other
not by the hundred nor by the thousand
but by the hundred thousand, here then
is Mr Iqbal with his remove class of
twenty Punjabis, some Sikh and some Muslim,
in a Secondary Modern School in London,
all of them trying to learn English.

Back home the fastidious guardians of freedom,
the Sikh army and the Muslim army, convinced
that East is East and West is West etcetera,
periodically accuse each other of aggression.

FOR THE LIBERATION OF BRAZIL

I.   *Lines for Álvares Cabral*

I take this land for Portugal
and command its native tribes to know
that in the name of King Manoel

I call this the Land of the Holy Cross.
I declare it married to Christ,
its souls his dowry.

Let this land be to Portugal
what the thighs of women are
to the eyes of lusting men.

Let this land give to Portugal
trees and precious stones
as a wife gives sons.

And in future ages let this land
be free from the repressive terror
of the jungle; let this land be free

from the tyranny of the savage:
let no man be afraid
of who might walk behind him.

II.   *The Arrival of the Slaves*

We were merchandise for the New World,
a commodity to be itemised
on a Bill of Lading, cargo to be unloaded
on the wharves of Rio and Bahia.

In the sugarcane fields we were
like bank-clerks who in one day
handle more money than they earn
in a lifetime of service.

Our women were merely loose
change for our Master to dice with;
our children were savings
he kept in reserve.

When the State decreed our freedom
the sun that shone like a silver coin
on our sweating black brows
was our only possession.

Lacking hard cash, should we now talk
of a golden future, we are put away
in sunless rooms as if again
we were in the ships that brought us here.

III.   *A Bad Summer in Rio*

Thunder knocks against the granite hills,
reverberating in the hollows of Rio;
such rain in these post-carnival weeks,
it's no time to be lying on the beaches.
    We stay indoors, play cards,
    grow accustomed to the rain.

Some friends telephoned from Leblon,
said they had taken the garden furniture
in and removed the swing from the courtyard,
compelling their disappointed children
    to stay indoors, play cards,
    grow accustomed to the rain.

The radio crackles. Many words are lost
in the transmission. The newspaper arrives
so bespattered with rain that its ink
has run, made whole paragraphs illegible.
    We're out of touch with the world,
    staying indoors, playing cards.

The gutters overflow with filth, the city stinks
as if it were a putrid carcase. Flies everywhere
with their bulging, complacent eyes. We're ruled
by anarchic storms which we silently witness,
    not sharing a comforting gossip,
    not joking about the weather.

High on the hills, above the mist,
thunder holds its assembly, a legislature
decreeing harsh laws, the helmeted sky
its militia compelling obedience,
    for the rain that began recently
    is as hard as bullets.

IV. *The Latest News*

Poor metaphor on crutches, slowly limping
through a tunnel towards the point of light!

Meanwhile the loud headlines declare
in a black fence across a field of newsprint

what the night before the reporter with the polka-dotted
bowtie despatched on videotape via satellite.

So, too, with the news from Brazil,
reminding me of the vultures flying above Rio,

the mud in Brasília beside the crown-of-thorns
cathedral and, from the drought-stricken North,

lorries loaded with emaciated peasants
creaking towards the oases of Rio and São Paulo.

The news will be obsolete tomorrow and like weapons
be dumped into some ocean of forgetfulness

and the reporter's face mourn another people's
tragedy. Meanwhile I labour at the same poem

wondering what metaphor can presume to describe
the pain of imprisoned students whose testicles

the police mutilate, whose minds the new
government likes to get into with electrical currents,

and wondering too, if the image is not
like a flower pressed between the closed pages of a book

or like the Brazilian prisoners
made extinct by a determined tyranny.